The Peer Counselor's

Pocket Book

By Joan Sturkie
and Valerie Gibson

RESOURCE PUBLICATIONS, INC.
San Jose, California

Editorial director: Kenneth Guentert
Book design: Christopher R. Gibson
Book production: Kent Zilliox
Cover design: Jim Lizardi
Cover production: Terri Ysseldyke-All

Reprint Department
Resource Publications, Inc.
160 East Virginia Street, Suite 290
San Jose, CA 95112-5848

Library of Congress Data
Sturkie, Joan, 1932-
    The peer counselor's pocketbook / by Joan Sturkie
and Valerie Gibson.
        p. cm.
    Includes bibliographical references.
    ISBN 0-89390-162-8
    1. Peer counseling—Handbooks, manuals, etc.
I. Gibson, Valerie. II. Title.
BF637.C6S79 1989
158'.3—dc20   89-10663 CIP

5   / 93 92

TABLE OF CONTENTS

DEDICATION

I dedicate this book to all of the peer counselors across the nation. This book is for you.

Joan

I dedicate this book to my mother, Carol Gibson, for her love, understanding, and encouragement. She gave me the support to write this book (my first book!), and the ability to move forward in my life. Thank you, Mom, I love you with all of my heart.

And to my dad, Robert W. Gibson. You are my role model, and I'm extremely proud to be the daughter of such a distinguished writer. I love you. And to Esme, who is a special part of my life.

A special thought to Chris Gibson and Paula Gibson. Thank you for always being there when I need you and giving me "sibling" advice, which I treasure more than you know.

Also, thank you to all my good friends, you know who you are. And a very special dedication, in memory of Eric Seyler, a former peer counselor and a special human being.

Valerie

ACKNOWLEDGMENTS

We gratefully acknowledge the help of the following people:

Christopher R. Gibson — for the design and layout of the book.

Carol Gibson— for editing and giving suggestions.

James Lizardi — for designing the book cover.

Jeff Cox, Rae Luce, and their peer counseling classes for offering valuable input.

INTRODUCTION

Congratulations, you are now a peer counselor! What exactly does that mean? It means you are a person who has been trained in communication skills, and you have learned how to apply them in helping another person with a personal or social problem. It also means you care about others and will take time to listen to their problems. Without giving advice, you will assist the person in managing and/or solving his or her own problems.

What responsibilities will you have?

1. To be available to the person needing help, whenever possible.

2. To listen.

3. To keep confidentiality.

4. To help the person solve his or her own problems.

5. To refer the person to a professional when warranted.

6. To report:

   Child abuse — to the department of social services or police.

   Potential suicide — to your leader, a professional, and/or a relative.

PURPOSE OF *THE PEER COUNSELOR'S POCKET BOOK*

This book is written by a peer counselor and a peer counseling teacher/trainer to fill a frequently expressed need for a quick, easy to read reference. It is written to give you a handy guide which may be readily available (jacket pocket or purse) and easily referred to for information or review. Since you are a trained peer counselor, some of the material may be familiar to you, but remembering all of it without a reminder (such as this book) may be difficult. The purpose of *The Peer Counselor's Pocket Book* is to make available to you a quick reference to reinforce those things which you learned but may have forgotten.

HOW TO USE *THE PEER COUNSELOR'S POCKET BOOK*

Place this book in your backpack, purse, or pocket of the clothing you are wearing so you will have it available when needed. You may need it occasionally or frequently, but not having it with you might be the exact time you will need it.

Turn to the Table of Contents and check which chapter applies to your problem. Sub-headings are listed for your convenience. In Chapter Five a space has been provided for you to add local telephone numbers as a referral service.

You will find this book to be most useful after you become thoroughly familiar with it and are able to find your answers quickly. We suggest you spend some time to fill in the telephone numbers and to become acquainted with the contents before you need the referral information.

CHAPTER 1

TIPS

RULES FOR COUNSELING PEERS

There are certain basic concepts you will always want to remember when you counsel a peer. These are generic in nature and will apply to any age person or any counseling situation. Review these tips daily until you find you use them as automatically as you do your toothbrush. As with any skill, improvement will come with practice.

- Be nonjudgmental.
- Be empathetic.
- Do not give advice.
- Do not take responsibility for the other person's problem.
- Stick with the here and now.
- Do not argue, verbally or nonverbally.
- Listen between the lines.
- Deal with the feelings first.
- Be genuine and sincere.
- Keep confidentiality.
- Be a vital part of a caring network.

MEETING A STRANGER

Remember, some people who need your help the most will not be those who will ask for it; the person sitting alone at lunchtime or the one standing alone at a social gathering may be feeling very lonely. This person may need your care and understanding as much as any of your counselees. It will be up to you to reach out to the stranger. You may do this by introducing yourself, starting a conversation, and listening to what the other person has to say. By using active listening, you will probably discover his or her needs and may be able to initiate future meetings to continue the helping relationship.

Steps for meeting a stranger:

1. Introduce yourself.
2. Initiate conversation which stems from the present surrounding and mutual interests.
3. Encourage the person to talk about himself or herself.
4. Be cautious about asking questions of a personal or intrusive nature. Show consideration for the person's privacy.
5. Listen attentively.
6. Use open-ended questions which usually begin with "How" or "What."
7. Show sincerity and respect to strangers.
8. Initiate appropriate closure which may include exchanging phone numbers or making plans to meet again.

CHAPTER 2

SKILLS

The word "skill" may be defined as an ability which is gained by knowledge and practice. To work effectively as a peer counselor, certain skills must be learned through this process. These skills are constantly improved and perfected as you put them to use.

Basic to all peer counseling will be skills in developing active listening, responding to counselees, sending effective messages, practicing values clarification/problem solving/decision making, and intervening in a crisis.

DEVELOPING ACTIVE LISTENING SKILLS

Characteristics of Active Listening

- Restate the person's most important thoughts and feelings.
- Be attentive. Don't daydream—keep your thoughts from wandering. Focus your thoughts on the person you are listening to.
- Convey understanding and acceptance by non-verbal behavior (posture, voice tone, eye contact, facial expression, gestures).
- Put yourself in the other's place to understand

what the person is saying, how he or she feels, and the values involved in the situation.

- Do not interrupt. Have patience—allow the person time to express his or her full thoughts and feelings.

- Do not offer advice or suggestions.

- Avoid bringing up similar feelings and problems from one's own experience.

- Develop the attitude that listening is fun and personally enriching.

- React appropriately. Applaud with nods, smiles, comments, and encouragements.

- Do not argue mentally with self-talk.

- Have a desire to listen. There is no such thing as uninteresting people—only disinterested listeners!

- Do not antagonize the speaker with hasty judgments.

- Listen for camouflaged feelings. Many times feelings are hiding behind words. Ask yourself what feelings you think you are hearing.

- Avoid changing the subject. Sometimes we get off-track and need to refocus on the actual issue.

Responses

- *Use open-ended questions.* Avoid questions requiring a "Yes" or "No" answer. Also remember to stay away from "Why" questions— these tend to put the counselee on the defensive. The counselee will feel the need to justify his or her behavior. Other words to beware of are "Did," "Have," and "Is." Good words to lead off a question with are "How" or "What."

- *Avoid making premature conclusions.* False assumptions invite erroneous conclusions.

- *Clarify the counselee's feelings, thoughts, and/or problems.* This will be helpful to both you and the counselee. Often the counselee needs to have what he or she has shared clarified. And sometimes it is important to have the counselee clarify something for you.

- *Focus on the counselee's feelings.* This shows you care about the counselee and offers validation of his or her feelings.

- *Do not be afraid to make a mistake.* It is O.K. to guess wrong about how the counselee feels or what he or she means. The counselee will appreciate your effort and attention.

- *Do not solve the counselee's problem.* It is important for the counselee to come to his or her own resolution. The counselee, through discovering his or her feelings and options, will be able to solve the problem himself or herself. In allowing the counselee this space, he or she will experience a feeling of adequacy and satisfaction.

- *Do not over-analyze.* This might cause the counselee to feel uncomfortable and to put up barriers.

- *Do not give "pat" answers.* Responses such as "Don't worry" or "Everyone goes through that" suggest what the person is feeling is unimportant. When someone is worried, he or she will not feel better after being told not to worry. If anything, the person will feel worse! It is necessary to validate, and help the counselee understand, his or her feelings.

- *Ask questions to help the counselee along.* Certain questions will aid the counselee to focus on the issue, look at it from a different perspective, and reveal information not already disclosed. In responding to your counselee, you might feel stumped on *how* to do it. What can I say after the counselee finishes talking? Some examples below might help you.

  - When asking questions:

    How are you feeling about that?
        or
    Can you tell me more about what happened?

  - When reflecting what the counselee shared:

    You seem angry about what they said...
        or
    You would like to see a change...

  - When conveying understanding:

    This must be very difficult for you.
        or
    That can really hurt.

- When clarifying:

    Are you saying it doesn't matter if she leaves?
       or
    It sounds like you're afraid of what they might do. Is that right?

- For summarizing:

    It sounds like you feel torn in the situation. You want to live with your Mom, but you don't want to hurt your Dad's feelings.

SENDING EFFECTIVE MESSAGES

Sending effective messages is important in peer counseling, and it is equally important in personal relationships. Certain guidelines will help you as you practice this skill.

- Use "I" statements for expressing feelings.

    Remember to "own" your feelings.
    → A correct example: "I am angry with you because... ."
    → An incorrect example: "You make me angry when you... ."

- Be congruent with verbal and non-verbal messages.

    Your body language should match your words.
    → A congruent example: A person says he or she feels fine, while a smile is on his or her face.

→ An incongruent example: A person says he or she feels fine, and a look of pain is on his or her face.

An incongruent message is often confusing because the receiver must decide whether to pay attention to the verbal or the non-verbal message.

- Communicate *caring* and *acceptance* of the receiver's feelings and reaction.

    Active listening may be used to respond to the receiver.

    → Examples: "I seem to be hearing you say the break-up with your boyfriend was not something you wanted. That must make it very painful."

    or

    → "It sounds like you are in a lot of pain because of the unwanted break-up with your boyfriend."

- Be specific.

    "You always..." or "You never..." are generalizations. It is important to tell someone an exact example of his or her behavior.

    → A correct example: "You cut classes four times last week."

    → An incorrect example: "You always cut classes."

- Include "want" statements in expressing what you would like someone to change.

    If the speaker does not convey explicit expectations in his or her message as to what is wanted, the receiver may perpetuate the personal dilemma, believing he or she is powerless to resolve the situation.

Asking Questions

In sending effective messages, there are three kind of questions used in communication. These are closed questions, open-ended questions, and "why" questions.

- "Closed" questions ask for specific information, such as: "Did you go to the store?" This type of questioning discourages the person from talking. Closed questions usually begin with "Is," "Did," or "Have" and are usually answered with a "Yes" or "No."

- "Open-ended" questions encourage conversation because feelings are allowed to be discussed. The most effective questions begin with "How" or "What."

- "Why" questions should be used infrequently because they often put the receiver on the defensive. Sometimes "why" questions make people feel they must explain or justify what has happened.

PRACTICING VALUES CLARIFICATION, PROBLEM SOLVING AND DECISION MAKING

Values clarification, problem solving, and decision making are all interrelated.

Values Clarification

Listed below are some guidelines to consider in values clarification:

- Active listening helps counselees express their feelings.
- Listen for what is important to the counselee.
- Restate to the counselee what you heard that seems important to him or her.
- Ask questions to help the counselee clarify what is important to him or her.
- Help the counselee verbalize one or two values in respect to his or her problem.
- Brainstorm some other values.

Problem Solving and Decision Making Model

Ten steps are generally recognized in effective problem solving and decision making:

1. *Clarify feelings* — use active listening to help the counselee sort out feelings. Making a list of these feelings may be helpful.

2. *Gather information* — find out as much as you possibly can about the situation.

3. *Define the problem* — what does the counselee perceive as the problem? Sometimes the first problem presented is not the primary one.

4. *Identify the decision* — what does he or she want to change?

5. *Brainstorm alternatives* — use open-ended, feeling-level questions to explore what the

real problem may be.

6. *Evaluate the alternatives* — list all possible solutions. Have the counselee prioritize the solutions in order of importance. Brainstorm the pros and the cons.

7. *Predict consequences* — discuss the outcome for each possible decision.

8. *Clarify values* — will certain decisions violate the counselee's values?

> Example: "The decision to have an abortion is not possible for me because I believe it is wrong."

9. *Make an action plan* — list the things which must be done first, second, and third to carry out the decision. Help the counselee make a plan for completing each step in a given amount of time.

10. *Follow-up* — make an appointment for the counselee to see you again and to report how the decision is working out for him or her. If it is not working well, start over. Use the ten steps again and arrive at a different decision.

CLARIFYING CONFLICTS AND FINDING RESOLUTIONS

A conflict may be defined as a disagreement, dispute, or quarrel. Students have a variety of conflicts in their lives. As a peer counselor, you will need to help the counselee recognize and deal with his or her conflict.

Conflicts may be internal, where the student is in conflict with himself or herself, or external, involving one or more people. The conflict also may be between a student and a collective entity, such as a school.

Conflicts may be resolved by:

1. Identifying the problem.
2. Listening to complaints.
3. Gathering information.
4. Seeking alternatives.
5. Making an action plan.
6. Reviewing the outcome.

INTERVENING IN A CRISIS

Situations which arise and threaten our psychological equilibrium may be defined as a crisis. These life events or situations may be expected or unexpected, real or imagined, actual or potential. During a crisis, a person becomes very vulnerable because basic human balance is disturbed.

Crises affect the physical body as well as the emotional being. It may be manifested in the form of:

- sweaty hands
- feeling of faintness
- racing heart
- change of body temperature
- shock
- vomiting

Prolonged physical responses may include:

- chronic fatigue
- allergies

- sleeping disorders
- migraine headaches
- gastrointestinal disorders
- heart problems

Steps for a peer counselor to follow when intervening in a crisis:

1. Provide the most appropriate level of protection, security, and nurturing, according to the person's obvious physical and mental needs.

2. Find out what the crisis is and what caused it.

3. Explore why the person cannot handle the current situation as he or she has done with other problems in the past.

4. Now that you know the problem, make certain the counselee also understands the situation and how it relates to him or her.

5. Explore alternative ways of coping with the problem and more positive ways of viewing the situation.

6. Lend appropriate support to the counselee's efforts at managing or resolving the problem.

7. Assist in the full recovery process toward a restored balance and/or an improved level of functioning.

Goals for the peer counselor involved in crisis counseling:

- Help the student cope effectively with the crisis situation and return to a normal state of

functioning as soon as possible.
- Follow-up after the crisis is over to see if the student is getting along satisfactorily.

The Chinese word for "crisis" involves two characters: one means danger; the other means opportunity. A student may see the crisis as a danger because he or she may be overwhelmed by the situation. It may also be viewed as an opportunity for the student to change and develop better ways of coping.

REMEMBER: AS WITH ANY SKILL, PEER COUNSELING IMPROVES WITH PRACTICE.

CHAPTER 3

COUNSELOR-COUNSELEE RELATIONSHIP

There are some essential elements involved in establishing and maintaining an honest, healthy counselor-counselee relationship. These include: initiating contact with the counselee, defining your role in the relationship, establishing trust, and being aware of certain boundaries. Each of these should be considered. Be conscious of them—they are important!

INITIAL CONTACT

- Introduce yourself and let the counselee know you are a peer counselor.
- Your first meeting with the counselee often feels uncomfortable—and that is O.K. This awkwardness will decrease with time.
- If initially you have problems getting the counselee to talk or open-up, share a *little* about yourself. Talk about whatever seems pertinent at the time.

DEFINE ROLE

- Ask why the counselee needs help. Why did he or she reach out to a peer counselor? How does this person feel about working with you? Often the counselee will be nervous, and asking how he or she feels about the situation may help release some of the anxiety.
- State the kind of help you can offer, relative to the problem he or she has.
- State your desire to help and to be available for the person.

ESTABLISH TRUST

- Assure the counselee of the confidentiality in the relationship. It is important, however, to let the counselee know there are particular things you need to report to authorities—such as child abuse or indications of a potential suicide or homicide.
- Discuss with the counselee how often you will meet. Beside the obvious necessity of arranging a time, this also reassures the counselee someone is there for him or her. This provides something consistent in the counselee's life, and a dependable friend.

BOUNDARIES

- As in any relationship, there are boundaries over which neither party should cross. As peer counselors, you are there to *listen*. You should not intrude into certain areas of the counselee's life unless they have given you permission to do so.

- You have boundaries also. And it may be necessary to establish these with the counselee. It is important to keep in mind that you are not responsible for the counselee's actions or feelings. Never feel guilty if things do not turn out right for the counselee.

THINGS TO BE AWARE OF

Being aware of boundaries may also help to prevent two different kinds of situations which will jeopardize the counselor-counselee relationship. One of these areas is when the counselor becomes the "rescuer." Another difficult situation may develop if the counselor and the counselee get attached to each other and become emotionally involved.

Do Not Rescue

As a peer counselor, your role is not to save the counselee. You are there to help him or her, help oneself. If you become a "rescuer" by taking care of something for the counselee, or by enabling him or her not to take risks, you are doing a disservice. You would cause harm to the counselee, and his or her personal growth, by assuming responsibilities which are not your own or by providing overprotection. In this respect, you would be violating the basic rules of peer counseling.

The Danger of Getting Attached

Getting attached can go either way. The counselee may develop a desire to become closer to you, or vice-versa. The desire may also be mutual. If you find you get along with the counselee and want to become socially and/or personally involved this is not necessarily wrong. But it is important for you to be aware that the counseling relationship will be sacrificed. No longer will you be an objective person—the purpose and needs in the counseling relationship will be clouded and displaced. You will have lost the emotional distance between you and the counselee which is essential in being a helpful peer counselor.

THINGS TO REMEMBER

- If in the counselor-counselee relationship stronger feelings become apparent, you must establish how you feel toward the counselee immediately. The counselee may need to work with a different peer counselor.
- If you find the counselee is becoming too dependent upon you, reestablish your boundaries, and talk with him or her about how you feel.
- When closing the counselor-counselee relationship, review the progress the counselee has made. Help the counselee recognize where he or she was when the counseling began and what has been accomplished since that time.

CHAPTER 4

SELF-AWARENESS

Self-awareness is a vital part of peer counseling. Peer counseling not only has to do with what the counselee is going through, but also with what is happening in your life. Being in touch with how you are feeling, or something you are experiencing, greatly affects how you can help a counselee. For example, if you have just had an argument with a friend and are now in a counseling session, chances are the fight will affect your nonverbal and verbal communication. The counselee will be able to sense something is wrong. If you are still feeling frazzled from the argument, you will be unable to be there for your counselee in a healthy way.

In a situation like this, there are some things you can do before and during your session with the counselee:

- First, try to calm yourself and focus on your feelings.
- If there is time before you meet with your counselee, seek out a peer and talk about how you are feeling.
- If you are still feeling upset, let the counselee know where you are coming from. You may feel more comfortable after being honest with

him or her. If you do not feel focused enough to be there for your counselee in a facilitative manner, ask the counselee if he or she would like to meet at another time. Sometimes this is not an option; at least communicate your feelings, thus, allowing you to be less distracted with your problem and better able to be a good listener.

Peer counselors, by no means, are without problems. Everyone experiences pain in his or her life. Peer counselors are human too. Through experiencing and working out problems we can listen more empathetically and be of greater value to the counselee. The peer counselor's function is to be a caring, understanding listener. How can you do that if you are unhealthily internalizing and running from your feelings?

When we keep our feelings in from family, friends, and counselees, it causes us to have displaced feelings. Be aware of what you are feeling and why. Be as honest as you can about your feelings—this will help prevent you from releasing your feelings in an inappropriate manner not only with a counselee, but others as well.

Self-awareness is an integral part of peer counseling for another important reason. Peer counselors are not "perfect"—we have problems too. If you are honest with yourself, sustain your self-awareness, and deal with your feelings, you will relate better to someone who is experiencing the same thing you did. For example, if you have a drinking problem and are in denial about it, or not seeking help for yourself, you may run into a problem when a counselee approaches you and he or she has a drinking problem. You may not recognize that the counselee has a problem. If the counselee specifically requests guidance in that area, and you have not dealt with or accepted your drinking problem, it is most likely you will not be clear-headed on the subject and able to give him or her the best information needed. Although, if you have recognized you have a problem and have sought help for yourself, you could be a tremendous help for your counselee. You will understand where he or she is coming from, and be able to share your own experience. The counselee will know that he or she is not alone and help is available.

The above situation is only one example. In practicing self-awareness there may be a whole array of problems to recognize and to resolve in your life: from school or work problems to serious family problems. It is very important to resolve those problems and deal with the feelings in a responsible, healthy way.

How to Check Your Self-Awareness:

- Be honest with yourself and others. Oftentimes we tend to internalize our feelings and act as if everything is O.K., when really, it is not. This can be very dangerous and lead to emotional instability.

- Recognize your feelings. Focus on those feelings.

- Don't run from whatever you may discover. Talk to someone about what you are feeling and what is happening in your life.

- Listen to others and their input.

- Do not discount or minimize your feelings— any feeling is important and deserves validation.

- Once you have recognized those feelings—deal with them in a healthy way. This may include a number of things; for example—resolving an argument or bad feelings about someone, seeking help for yourself, or writing down your feelings for even further release. The list is endless once you put your mind to it.

QUESTIONS TO ASK YOURSELF

There are questions you might consider asking yourself after you have met with a counselee. These questions may help you reflect back on your session to discover areas of your skills which you may want to work on. It may also help shed some light on your counselee's problem and reveal how you can be most helpful to him or her.

Concerning Active Listening:

- Did I focus solely on the counselee?
- How was my body language?
- Did I respond with appropriate nonverbal communication?
- Did I refrain from giving advice?
- Did I refrain from passing judgment?
- Did I allow the counselee time to completely express his or her thoughts and feelings?
- Did I restate (reflect) the counselee's feelings?
- Was I able to uncover feelings the counselee was hiding behind words?
- Was I empathetic?

- Did I put myself in the counselee's shoes to understand how he or she was feeling?
- Did we stick with the issue at hand?
- Did I refrain from arguing with the counselee?
- Was I supportive?
- Did I express caring and love?

Checking Responses:

- Did I validate the counselee's feelings?
- Was I able to ask questions which helped the counselee to further express his or her feelings?
- Did I do anything which caused the counselee to put up barriers?
- Did I avoid over-analyzing?
- Did I refrain from expressing my opinion?
- Did I use open-ended questions?
- Was I able to clarify and summarize the counselee's thoughts and feelings?

About the Counselee's Problem:

- What feelings did the counselee express?
- What is the issue being dealt with?
- Is this a problem I need to report to the proper authorities? (If unsure, always check with your supervisor.)

- Did the counselee seem to feel better after the session?
- If we did not arrange another time to meet— do I need to try to meet with the counselee again?

General Questions:

- Am I feeling guilty about something involving the counselee? Remember—you are not responsible for the counselee's problems or feelings, *never feel guilty.*
- Am I comfortable with the problem the counselee needs to work on?
- Do my values get in the way of my objectivity on this particular issue?
- Do I need to discuss the counselee's problem with my supervisor?
- Does this problem require a referral?
- Do I have any irritating habits I need to change (interrupting, daydreaming, poor body language, etc.)?
- What can I do differently next time to better help a counselee?

CHAPTER 5

REFERRALS

You are trained and able to counsel peers, but there will be times when your counselee will need professional help. Do not feel inadequate when the situation is beyond your capabilities. You have already performed an important task by helping the counselee to identify the problem and to see the need for contacting another person. When you have accomplished this, you will then act as a "bridge" to professional help. Remember to let your counselee know that you are still available for support while he or she is receiving additional help. It is also important to be available for the counselee when the outside help has been completed. The professional counselor may ask for your assistance after discharging the client. This help would come in the form of alerting the professional if things start to go downhill again for the student. This is particularly true of students who have previously attempted suicide.

WHEN TO REFER:

As a peer counselor, you should refer a counselee when you lack the skill/experience/knowledge, emotional stamina, or time to begin or continue counseling.

Seek outside help when your counselee is:

- requiring medical attention
- showing aggressive behavior
- abusing drugs
- talking about suicide
- being physically, sexually, or emotionally abused (child abuse)
- appearing to be emotionally unstable
- asking for professional help
- having a legal problem

If there is ever a question of whether to refer or not, ask your peer counseling teacher or the person supervising you for guidance. When in doubt, do not linger about making a decision. Check with someone immediately.

WHERE TO REFER

Peer counselors need to be familiar with agencies and persons in the community to whom they may refer their counselees. The list of referrals may include psychiatrists, psychologists, marriage, family and child counselors, suicide prevention centers, physicians, Alcoholics Anonymous, child abuse agencies, and departments of public social services.

For your convenience, a list of some referral places are given below. You will need to write the local phone numbers on the lines provided.

Where to refer when your counselee has a problem relating to:

AIDS:
AIDS information (local)   _____
Hospital   _____
(Other)   _____

Alcoholism:
Alcoholics Anonymous (local)   _____
Alateen, Alanon headquarters   _____
Alateen, Alanon (local)   _____
Chemical dependency hospital   _____
(Other)   _____

Child Abuse:
Child Abuse Hotline   _____
Public Social Services Department
(Child Welfare Office)   _____
Police   _____
(Other)   _____

Depression, anxiety, confusion:
Mental health clinic   _____
Private psychiatrist, psychologist,
or licensed counselor   _____
(Other)   _____

Drug Problems:
Alcoholics Anonymous (local)   _____
Narcotics Anonymous (local)   _____
Cocaine Anonymous (local)   _____
Drug abuse treatment center   _____
(Other)   _____

Eating Disorders:
Overeaters Anonymous   _____
Private clinic   _____
Psychologist or other mental
health professional   _____
Anorexia and bulimia specialist   _____
(Other)   _____

Financial Matters:
Local welfare office   _____
United Fund Office   _____
Local church   _____
(Other)   _____

Handicap:
Society for the Blind   _____
Crippled Children's Society   _____
(Other)   _____

Legal Problems:
Legal Aid Society   _____
Local attorney   _____
(Other)   _____

Marriage Problems:
Marriage, Family, and Child
Counselor (local)   _____
Psychologist or other mental
health professional   _____
Shelter for abused wives   _____
Local clergy   _____
(Other)   _____

Missing Person:
Police Department _____
(Other) _____

Physical Problem:
Doctor's office (local) _____
Hospital (local) _____
(Other) _____

Poisoning:
Poison Control Center _____
(Other) _____

Pregnancy:
Doctor's office (local) _____
Planned Parenthood (local) _____
Home for unwed mothers _____
Social Services Department _____
(Other) _____

Rape:
Rape Hotline _____
Hospital _____
Police _____
Mental health professional _____
(Other) _____

Spiritual Problem:
Church (various ones, local) _____
Additional church _____
(Other) _____

Suicide Threat or Attempt:

Suicide Hotline   _____

Suicide prevention center   _____

Mental health clinic   _____

Psychiatrist, Psychologist,
or other mental health person   _____

Hospital (local)   _____

(Other)   _____

STEPS IN REFERRING

1. Be familiar with community resources so you can refer to the most appropriate place and/or person.

2. Before referring, check with the referral source to be certain that your counselee can be accepted for help.

3. Tell your counselee why you feel he or she needs to be referred.

4. Indicate to the counselee your reason for each particular referral recommendation you've shared with him or her.

5. Try to involve your counselee in the decision to refer.

6. Let your counselee make his or her own appointment, if possible. You may not have the necessary information needed for scheduling the appointment.

7. If warranted, help the counselee plan how he or she will get to the appointment and determine if another person is needed to go along.

8. Keep an interest in the counselee even after he or she has been referred. Be ready to support the counselee during and after the time he or she is seeing a professional. Let the counselee know you care.

MANDATORY REPORTING TO AUTHORITIES

By law, all cases of child abuse must be reported. This includes physical, emotional, or sexual abuse. Do not feel that something happened too long ago to report it. Report the incident no matter when it occurred. Let the authorities determine if it should be pursued.

Suicide, or the intent to do bodily harm, should always be reported to your supervisor and to the person (parent) who is legally responsible for your counselee.

REMEMBER: IT IS IMPORTANT AND O.K. TO REC-OGNIZE YOUR LIMITATIONS WHEN COUNSEL-ING SOMEONE AND TO ASK FOR HELP FROM YOUR SUPERVISOR, ANOTHER PEER COUNSELOR, OR A PROFESSIONAL.

CHAPTER 6

COVERING THE ISSUES

SUICIDE

Suicide is the voluntary act of taking one's own life. It represents a failure in communication between the individual and his or her meaningful relationships, together with an inability to cope with the stresses of life.

Suicide is an act of desperation. It truly is a "dropout" from life which is permanent. Suicide is a permanent solution to a temporary problem.

As a peer counselor, you need to take every mention of suicide seriously.

Adolescent suicide and suicide attempts constitute a major problem in the United States today. The present suicide rate for young people has doubled in the last decade and tripled in the last twenty years, while the nation's overall suicide rate has not varied much in the past half-century.

Usually suicidal adolescents are looking at their world through a very narrow perspective. They say things like, "I've tried everything and nothing works" or "I can't handle it anymore." In reality, they have probably tried very few alternatives. As a peer counselor, you will want to enlarge the perspective for these young people and help them find other alternatives.

Stressful situations that can trigger suicidal feelings:

- Depression which has not been recognized or treated.
- Major life changes, such as death of a parent or friend, school failure, divorce, or break-up with a boyfriend or girlfriend.
- Illness which may be prolonged or terminal.
- Use or abuse of drugs and alcohol.

Suicide attempts:

- More women than men attempt suicide.
- Men often use more violent methods. Women tend to use barbiturates, other drugs or poisons, while men often use guns.

Suicides which are completed:

- More men than women kill themselves.
- Anyone may commit suicide, at any age.

Danger signs to look for in the potentially suicidal person:

- *Previous attempts* — if the person has attempted suicide before, he or she may be at high risk to try again. The person may talk about previous suicide attempts without saying he or she is considering it at the present time.
- *Threats* — if the counselee is threatening to commit suicide, the peer counselor must always take such threats seriously. Experts in the field of suicide estimate that threats are followed by suicide attempts at least seventy percent of the

time. The counselee may not say he or she is going to kill himself or herself, but the words may be something like, "I'm not planning to be around much longer."

- *Extreme depression* — if the counselee appears to be extremely depressed or has had changes in personality or behavior, the peer counselor will want to look into this further. The counselee's depression may be exhibited by a loss of weight, inability to sleep, or a tendency to withdraw. Loneliness is a major factor in suicide.

- *Changes in personality or behavior* — if the person has been depressed previously, and all of a sudden seems to be happy and appears to have had a burden lifted, the peer counselor should probe into what has happened. Sometimes a sudden shift in moods may mean that he or she is relieved because a plan for suicide has been made. The counselee may believe the pain of living will soon come to an end.

- *Preparation for death* — if the counselee is preparing for death, this is a signal which should alert the peer counselor to possible danger ahead. The counselee may start talking about giving away favorite possessions, making a will, or buying a gun.

Ways a peer counselor can help:

- *Be alert to what the real problem is.* Listen for what the counselee is not saying, as well as what is being said.

- *Let the person know you take him or her seriously.*

- *Listen to the person and follow-up with appropriate*

questions. If the signs are apparent, you may ask the person if he or she is thinking about suicide. You may ask if the person has a plan, how that plan would be carried out, and if pills or guns are available. Remember, mentioning suicide does not give the counselee the idea. A suicidal person already has the idea, and talking about it openly may help to prevent the counselee from acting out the suicide.

- *Do not argue or try to reason.* Never tell the counselee, "You can't kill yourself because... ."

- *Explore other options with the counselee.* He or she may not realize that other options are available.

- *Tell the person help is available.*

- *Refer the counselee to a professional or a suicide prevention service.* Many people have had extensive training in suicide prevention and are experts in the field.

- *Stay close to the person until professional help is available.*

Common Misconceptions About Suicide:

- False: If someone wants to kill himself or herself you can't stop it from happening.

  True: Most suicidal gestures or attempts are a cry for help, which the person cannot communicate by other means.

- False: People who talk about killing themselves seldom do.

True: The majority of persons attempting suicide have talked about it. Suicide threats and attempts must be taken seriously.

- False: The tendency toward suicide is inherited and passed on from one generation to another.

  True: Suicide does not "run in families." It has no genetic quality.

- False: The suicidal person wants to die and feels there is no turning back.

  True: Suicidal persons most often reveal ambivalence about living versus dying and frequently call for help immediately following the suicide attempt.

- False: Only a certain type of person commits suicide.

  True: Suicide occurs in all social classes, races, religions, in all personality types and all levels of intelligence.

- False: Everyone who commits suicide is depressed.

  True: Although depression is often associated with suicidal feelings, not all people who kill themselves are obviously depressed. Some of these people are anxious, agitated, psychotic, or simply feel they can not deal with their life situation and want to escape.

- False: Suicidal persons rarely seek medical help.

  True: In retrospective studies of people who had committed suicide, more than half had sought medical help within the six months preceding the suicide.

- False: If you ask a client directly, "Do you feel like killing yourself?" that will lead him or her to make a suicide attempt.

  True: Asking a counselee directly about suicidal intent will often minimize the anxiety surrounding the feeling and act as a deterent to the suicidal behavior.

- False: A suicide attempt means that person will always think of attempting it again.

  True: Often a suicide attempt is made during a particularly stressful period. If the remainder of that period is appropriately managed, the person will go on with his or her life.

- False: It takes courage for a person to commit suicide.

  True: Suicide is often seen as the only way to relieve the pain. It is not an act of courage, but an act of desperation.

REMEMBER: BE ALERT AND LISTEN. SOMEONE
MAY BE TALKING ABOUT SUICIDE AND YOU
COULD POSSIBLY BE THE ONLY ONE WHO WILL
HEAR THE CRY FOR HELP.

SELF-ESTEEM

Self-esteem is a feeling of personal self-worth. People
who have high self-esteem feel good about themselves,
while those with low self-esteem usually find life to be
unfulfilling.

As a peer counselor, you will want to help your
counselees develop confidence and courage to face their
situations. Many problems which will be presented to
you will result from the person having low self-esteem.
Any way you can help the person to raise his or her self-
esteem will fortify the counselee against future potential
problems. However, this process must come from within
each individual. It is not derived from external sources.
No one can create this experience except the individual
himself. You, as a peer counselor, can be there to listen
and support while the process is taking place.

The importance of supporting a counselee in his or
her goal to raise self-esteem cannot be overstated. Healthy
self-esteem gives a person the ability to respond to the
opportunities of life in an active and positive way. You
can make a difference in a counselee's life by helping that
person realize how important self-worth really is.

CHILD ABUSE

Child abuse is an act of non-accidental injury or any
omission or commission which interferes with a child's
development. Child abuse usually means physical injuries inflicted on children by their caretakers, however, it

also means emotional abuse. Child neglect is failure of the caretakers to provide adequate nurturance, protection or supervision. Child molesting refers to sexual abuse of children by adults.

Child abuse may be:

- *Physical abuse* — an act that does harm to a child's body. It may result in bruises, burns, fractures or dislocations, or internal injuries.

- *Emotional abuse*— a verbal act which damages a child's mental and emotional health. This may be done by belittling, screaming, threatening, blaming, or using sarcasm.

- *Sexual abuse*— an act of sexually mistreating a child, either directly by forcing or coercing sexual contact with a child, or indirectly through exposure to pornography.

The abused child may try to cope by becoming:

- *Passive* — he or she will maintain a low profile by trying to stay out of sight. This child hopes to avoid contact with his or her parents and may also avoid other adults, thinking they may be abusive too.

- *Responsible* — older children may take on parenting roles. They will take care of the younger children and do the cooking and cleaning on a regular basis.

- *Disruptive*— this child cannot seem to get along with peers or adults. He or she may be aggressive and get into fights often. This person may intentionally provoke adults and get them angry because it is the only way he or she knows how to interact with others.

Example of a child abuse law, in part:

The California Child Abuse Law

Statute: California Penal Code §11161.5

Definition of a Child: Any person under the age of 18 years.

Nature of Injuries That Must Be Reported: (1) Physical injury or injuries which appear to have been inflicted by other than accidental means by any person: (2) sexual molestation: (3) injuries suffered as a result of any person who, under circumstances or conditions likely to produce great bodily harm or death, or under circumstances other than those likely to produce great bodily harm or death, willfully caused or permitted any child to suffer; or, who inflicted thereon unjustifiable pain or mental suffering; or, having the care or custody of any child, willfully caused or permitted the person or health of such child to have been injured; or, willfully caused or permitted such child to be placed in such situation that its person or health was endangered.

Suggestions for the peer counselor:

- *Listen patiently* — remember the abused person will have feelings of guilt, shame, and helplessness. He or she may be hesitant to admit the abuse because there is a feeling that somehow the abuse is his or her fault.

- *Support the abused* — he or she may feel guilty about what has happened and also helpless to change the situation.
- *Be nonjudgmental* — show empathy and concern.
- *Refer to proper mental health professionals* — because of the emotional trauma of any abuse, the counselee will probably need long-term professional help.
- *Report all abuse or suspected abuse to the proper authorities.* We suggest you first discuss this with your supervisor.

REMEMBER: AS A PEER COUNSELOR, YOU WILL REPORT ALL SUSPICIONS OF CHILD ABUSE.

FAMILY PROBLEMS

For family problems we cover divorce, parent/child communication breakdown, and conflict with stepparents. These are only a few of the issues which may be experienced by teens and their families, and they have been simplified for better understanding. Many problems are interconnected, and each is unique to the individual. Even though we discuss only three of the many family issues which exist, you will have a good foundation to deal with any other problems that a counselee may bring to you.

Divorce

When someone's family is getting a divorce, the most important thing a peer counselor can do is listen. The counselee will have many painful and conflicting feelings. These feelings need to be addressed and released for the counselee to begin the healing process. Your main function is to listen lovingly and to offer support.

A large percentage of peer counselors have experienced a divorce in their family. In this capacity, if you are from a divorced family, you will be able to relate to the feelings expressed and may want to share some of your own experience and feelings on a limited basis. Remember you are there to give your undivided attention to the counselee. Be selective in choosing times to share your own feelings. Letting the counselee know they are not alone or different can be very therapeutic—just remember to use your discretion.

Whether or not you have personally felt the pains of divorce, your support for the counselee will be extremely helpful to him or her. What this person needs most is someone to listen—someone who is available for him or her.

Here are some feelings and characteristics to be aware of while counseling teenagers who are going through a family separation:

- *anger* — they are losing something meaningful to them. Anger may be at one parent or both parents. Remember, anger is always an indication of pain.
- *hurt* — the family is breaking up. A parent is leaving the teenager, and family unity is being severed. The divorce is not just happening to the parents.
- *lonely* — often teenagers are ignored by their parents during this time. Many parents, because of the pain they are experiencing, do not consider the pain the children are going through.

- *confusion* — they are experiencing the agony of balancing their loyalty to each parent.
- *disillusionment* — they wonder: Why is this happening? What went wrong? Why me?
- *isolation* — this is a reaction from the upset in family life and thus their personal life. A tendency to isolate themselves from family and friends is common. Teenagers experiencing divorce in their family may not want to open up about how they are feeling. They may not allow others into their personal world of confusion and pain.
- *guilt* — teenagers often assume responsibility for the divorce.
- *stressed out* — teenagers already have a lot of stress. The added strain of divorce may be more than they can handle.
- *low self-worth* — this becomes an issue particularly if they feel responsible for the divorce. They feel as though they are not *worth* enough for their parents to keep the family together; somehow they are at fault.

Parent/Child Communication Breakdown

Expressions such as, "My parents just don't understand" or "You're just a kid, you aren't mature enough yet…" are classic examples symptomatic of communication breakdown between teens and their parents. When communication is not open and free in a family setting, when yelling or just not talking is the norm, the result is an extremely unhealthy environment. This environment may be the reason for a teen experiencing school problems, feeling angry or depressed, abusing alcohol and drugs, or acting out rebelliously. Once these problems have surfaced, the lack of healthy communication in a family will serve as a catalyst, making the problems worse.

Usually a counselee will not approach you seeking counseling specifically because of a communication problem with his or her parents. Many teenagers may not recognize there is a communication problem in their family, because this is what they have lived with all of their life. You will discover that communication breakdown in the family is often an underlying symptom of another issue. Unfortunately, lack of good communication is almost an epidemic when it comes to teens and parents. Neither the teen nor the parent is to blame, although each is responsible for his or her own behavior.

Support you may offer teens who are suffering from communication breakdown with their parents:

- Listen.
- Help the counselee explore the option of learning how to send effective messages.
- Role play a family situation, allowing the counselee to be both the teen and the parent. This helps the counselee to view his or her behavior from a new perspective, and see how he or she contributes to the family dynamics. The counselee will also be able to better understand where his or her parents are coming from. Role playing will help prepare the counselee for communication situations and hopefully for confronting the parents about how he or she is feeling.
- Help the counselee understand the importance

of taking care of himself or herself. The counselee needs to see what changes need to be made in his or her own communication skills and behavior.

- Check in with the counselee on a regular basis to talk about any progress which is being made. Help the counselee examine what he or she could have done differently and provide positive reinforcement. It is important for the counselee to receive affirmation for what he or she is doing and encouragement for the risks being taken.

- Problems which coincide with the communication breakdown also need to be addressed. Often it is too unclear to know which problem caused the other to exist. Many times these problems overlap; you and the counselee will need to decide which one to work on.

Conflict with Stepparents

When parents get remarried, sometimes the children will resent the stepparent. They may feel as though the stepparent is an intruder into their family unit. Or they may feel as if the stepparent is trying to be "Mom" or "Dad."

Suggestions for the peer counselor:

- *Listen to the counselee, using your active listening skills.*

- *Express caring and acceptance.*

- *Role play.* Help the counselee express what he or she is feeling toward the parents and the stepparent. Role playing will help the counselee to clarify and work on his or her feelings.

- *Work on how to send effective messages.* The counselee needs to recognize his or her behavior which contributes to conflict with the stepparent.

- *Set objectives and goals with the counselee.* An example of this is the use of sending effective messages in communicating with the stepparent and/or parents about how he or she is feeling.

DEATH AND DYING

Death touches every person at some time or another, and in your role as a peer counselor, you will be called upon to be available for a counselee who has experienced such a loss. If the death is in the family, the counselee may not want to talk to other family members, thinking he or she might put an added burden on them. A peer counselor can play an important role for the counselee at this time.

- The experience of grief is felt by every person at some point during a lifetime.

- Grief is an experience of anxiety and depravation which can manifest itself physically, emotionally, socially, and spiritually.

- Any loss can bring about grief: death of another person, divorce, death of a pet, retirement from one's job, selling a home, or moving away from friends and neighbors.

- Whenever a part of life is removed there is grief.

Granger Westburg, the author of *Good Grief* has identified several stages of grief. These stages may overlap and merge with each other:

- shock
- emotional release
- depression/loneliness
- physical distress
- panic
- guilt
- hostility/resentment
- inability to return to usual activities
- gradual hope
- struggles to affirm reality

Ways peer counselors can help the person who is grieving:

- Encourage discussion about death before it occurs.
- Be available after the person returns from the funeral and after everyone else has gone. Often times many people are available at the funeral and for the next week thereafter. Usually by the second week friends are back to their normal routines, and the person who is grieving is alone. This is when the peer counselor may be most needed.
- Make it known that expressing feelings is good and acceptable. However, do not pressure the griever to show feelings.
- Expect the griever to be emotionally upset and let him or her know you are still available.
- Be a receptive listener.

- Provide practical help in the beginning. Free the person, allowing him or her to have time to grieve.
- Participate in grieving rituals, such as funerals or memorial services.

The peer counselor may learn that the counselee has found out that he or she has a terminal illness. Because peers feel comfortable talking to peers, you may be the one who the dying person reaches out to. In order to best relate to this person, you need to know and understand what he or she may be feeling and experiencing.

Fears the dying person may have:
- *The fear of the unknown.* The counselee may wonder if "this is all there is" or if there is a life beyond this one.
- *The fear of losing the opportunities and goals of a lifetime.* When young people find out they will not be able to live their life out fully, there is often a feeling of loss and sometimes a feeling of being cheated out of what might have been.
- *The fear that after they are dead everyone will get along fine without them.* A young girl may want to talk about her sister moving into her room after she is gone; a boy may want to talk about his younger brother taking his place on the football team. Feeling that someone will take their place and they will not be missed is a real fear for many people.
- *The fear of pain.* The counselee may be wondering how much pain will come before death. His or her own ability to withstand pain also may be a concern.

- *The fear of being left alone.* The counselee may wonder if the family will have time to make frequent hospital visits. Will death come when no one else is there?

In her book *On Death and Dying*, Elizabeth Kubler-Ross talks about the stages a dying person may go through before the end of life. The peer counselor should know these stages:

1. *Denial* — the person may refuse to believe that he or she is dying. This stage may vary in length, with some people staying in it longer than others. It is a temporary stage, but it may surface again at any time.

2. *Anger* — the counselee may question why this is happening. When the answer is not apparent, he or she may lash out in anger at the seemingly unfairness of it all. At the same time, the counselee may feel guilty for feeling angry.

3. *Bargaining* — this is usually an attempt to postpone death. The peer counselor may not be aware of this stage, since the dying person often does not tell anyone. The bargaining is usually done in secret, often with God.

4. *Depression* — when the dying person faces the reality of his or her death, depression often sets in. It may come when symptoms of terminal illness become impossible to ignore. The counselee may express to the peer counselor his or her feelings of despair.

5. *Acceptance* — when the dying person works through the feelings and conflicts that have arisen, he or she may now be ready to accept the

fact that death will soon come. The peer counselor will recognize this as being a time of
emotional calm. The counselee will have reached
a state of peace.

What the peer counselor can do for the dying counselee:

- *Spend time with the person.* Because this may take
more time than is normally spent with each
counselee, the peer counselor should be careful
not to overextend himself or herself. This may
include limiting the number of people you
counsel.

- *Listen patiently.* The counselee may want to talk
through many different issues.

- *Avoid reacting negatively to the counselee during the
anger stage.* Some days the counselee may appear to be angry and may direct that feeling
toward the peer counselor. By realizing anger is
a normal feeling for a dying person, the peer
counselor should not take the words personally.

- *Explore options with the counselee.* Sometimes the
person may feel there are no options available in
the months ahead. When he or she has realized
options do exist in the life that is left, the acceptance of death will be easier.

- *Let the counselee know you care.* Having the knowledge that someone cares and is there for him or
her will make a difference to most people.

EATING DISORDERS

Why are we discussing eating disorders? Because it is a serious issue among teenagers, particularly young women. It has always been present, but not until recently has more been revealed about this disorder, the incredible extent of the problem, the acceptance from society that it is real and very serious, and the steps one can take to recover.

Individuals with an eating disorder feel that if they could lose weight everything would be better. They lose perspective on how they really appear. They have an image of themselves different than how others see them.

At first, the individual with an active eating disorder is happy about how he or she appears. The person will become more self-confident in school and social activities. As the eating disorder progresses the individual increasingly focuses on weight and control of food. What follows is lowered self-esteem, isolation, lack of communication with family and friends, and other symptoms which are listed below. Remember, a person need not exhibit all of these symptoms to qualify as having an eating disorder.

General description of an eating disorder: an abnormal eating pattern, usually resulting from emotional or psychological problems which may produce serious physiological consequences.

Types of eating disorders:

- *Anorexia nervosa* — self-induced starvation. People with anorexia nervosa have a fear of eating. They have a distorted view of their appearance. These individuals may feel they are fat when in reality they are very thin. Anorexia nervosa is an extremely dangerous eating disorder and can result in death.

- *Bulimia (bulimarexia)*—binging and purging for weight control. Individuals with bulimia eat large amounts of food uncontrollably and eliminate it through vomiting, diuretics, or laxatives. They view their behavior as a way to enjoy food without experiencing weight gain. This develops into a very serious dependency involving much more than weight consciousness.
- *Overeating* — eating compulsively to escape reality and numb feelings. The overeater is using food to "fix it." This disorder is similar to other obsessive compulsive disorders.

Symptoms

Characteristics associated with eating disorders:
- over-achievement
- perfectionism

Behavior associated with eating disorders:
- preoccupation with food
- unusual eating patterns
- isolating after meals
- obsessive behavior
- social isolation — withdrawal
- drop in grades

Feelings associated with eating disorders:
- low self worth
- depression
- irritability

- anxiousness
- radical mood and personality changes
- inability to concentrate
- not verbalizing thoughts and feelings as often as usual

Obvious physical symptoms associated with eating disorders:

- rapid weight loss or gain
- unattractively and unhealthily thin
- protruding hips
- eyes are watery, bloodshot, and/or have circles
- broken blood vessels in facial area — results from vomiting
- red, dry cracked lips
- gum chewing — to cover up the smell from vomiting

Not-as-obvious physical symptoms associated with eating disorders:

- dry mouth
- susceptibility to colds
- constipation
- irregular menstrual periods
- weakness and fatigue
- laxative dependence

Steps for helping someone with an eating disorder:

1. When the counselee is in denial about his or her disorder, and you are recognizing serious symptoms, talk to your supervisor. Eating dis-

orders pose dangerous health threats and should not be minimized or ignored.

2. Remember to use your active listening skills.

3. Help the counselee to look at the effects of his or her disorder. If the counselee is in denial, he or she may become defensive. Use your judgment and keep in mind the detrimental effects of eating disorders.

4. When the counselee has admitted to having a problem, listen to the feelings expressed.

5. Let the counselee know there is help and that he or she is not alone.

6. Discuss the options for recovery with the counselee.

7. Ask what he or she would like to do.

8. Make the appropriate referral.

Where to refer the counselee:

- Overeaters Anonymous — for an overeater, bulimic, or anorexic

- Weight loss program

- Hospital unit specializing in eating disorders— primarily for an anorexic or bulimic.

- Eating disorder specialist (any known professional specializing in eating disorders).

- Counselor, psychologist, psychotherapist, or psychiatrist.

SCHOOL PROBLEMS

Many of the counselees who come to you will be experiencing school problems. The primary problem could be related to school or the result of another issue. School problems may include a number of things: attendance, tardiness, grades, conflict with teachers, or a rebellious attitude toward school and authority in general. Most likely it will be a combination of two or more problems.

Clarifying and specifying the problem is essential when helping a counselee with school troubles. When a student is having problems, the situation tends to be confusing and unclear to him or her. The student often feels overwhelmed; when an individual is struggling in one area at school, all other areas will be affected. This causes tremendous stress and feelings of hopelessness.

You may be able to attempt to help your counselee focus on a specific problem in order to create an actual starting point for working on his or her situation. This will help relieve some of the stress which the counselee is experiencing.

Keep in mind that troubles in school are often an indicator of another underlying problem; for example, family problems, alcohol and drug use, or low self-esteem.

Steps to follow in helping the counselee with school problems:

Define the problem:
- Ask the counselee what he or she feels the problem is.
- Help the counselee clarify the specific problem(s).

For example, if the problem is in a certain class, have the counselee pinpoint exactly what is troubling to him or her.

- Active listening skills are essential in aiding the counselee to define the problem.

Make up a plan:

1. Specify an area of school performance to work on (i.e. attendance, grades).

2. With the counselee, establish a realistic goal he or she would like to achieve.

3. Establish short-term objectives as part of the plan; for example, the counselee will attend English five days in a row or will turn in a specific assignment on time.

4. Discuss and write down the steps to take in achieving the established goal. It is important to remember not to take on too much at once. Small, gradual steps may be necessary to build self-confidence, and to prevent failure from taking on so much that the counselee becomes discouraged and gives up.

5. Discuss how often, where, and at what time you and the counselee will meet to check progress and talk about how the counselee is feeling.

Discuss the outcome:

- Have the counselee discuss the pros and the cons of his or her present behavior and of the goal which has been established.

- Have the counselee discuss what behavior he or she wants to change.

Check counselee's progress:

- Give positive reinforcement for the progress the counselee has made.
- Offer support and empathy.

PEER PRESSURE

Much of the social pressure teens receive is from people who attend school with them. Peer pressure causes teens to do things they do not want to do, but they will do it to be "one of the crowd," to fit in, to feel liked and accepted. One of the most typical situations is when other teens pressure another into drinking or using drugs. Another common peer pressure problem is teens being pressured into having sex.

The unfortunate thing about peer pressure situations is that it is often the beginning of a cycle, not just a one-time incident. Once teens have been pressured into doing something they do not feel right about, it becomes less difficult the following time to repeat the behavior. Soon they will be the ones pressuring a peer. This is not true of all peer pressure situations, but it is extremely common.

How to help a counselee work through peer pressure:

- Let the counselee know he or she is special. It is important to reinforce the unique and likeable qualities the counselee has.
- Work with the counselee on clarifying his or her values. This will help the counselee draw boundaries between what others value and what he or she truly wants for oneself.
- Help the counselee build his or her self-esteem. Each person must gain self-esteem to have a

better sense of doing what he or she wants, instead of trying to please others in order to feel good about himself or herself. When someone acts against his or her own values and beliefs in order to be accepted, the person's self-esteem is never built up, only cheated.

- Work with the counselee on being assertive so that in a peer pressure situation he or she can learn to:
  - → express what he or she wants to do
  - → express how he or she feels about the situation
  - → be honest, using a firm and direct tone
  - → be respectful of others in the situation
  - → be spontaneous in expressing feelings, trying not to hesitate
  - → accept responsibility for the feelings expressed

- Role play with the counselee, emphasize assertive techniques (the ones mentioned above are only a few suggestions; do not close the door on any other ideas). Remember to reinforce the counselee's own values.

- Remind the counselee that no one will ostracize him or her for doing what he or she feels is best. If anything, the counselee may discover that his or her new behavior will elicit respect. If not, the other people involved obviously have some issues to work on themselves.

REMEMBER: YOU WILL FREQUENTLY ENCOUNTER COUNSELEES WITH SCHOOL PROBLEMS. EXPERIENCE WILL SERVE TO BE A USEFUL TOOL.

YOU WILL BE ABLE TO OFFER EMPATHY AND
SUPPORT. TRUST YOUR INSTINCTS AND LISTEN!

SUBSTANCE ABUSE

The term "substance abuse" encompasses the use of
both alcohol and drugs. Most teenagers experiment with
these substances; some of these teens may develop a
temporary problem; others will not like the effects; and
some will become addicted. Alcoholism is a disease.
Young as well as older people become afflicted with it.

During your experience as a peer counselor, you
likely will find students coming to you with school
related problems or feelings of depression. Many of
these teenagers actually have a more serious underlying
problem: substance abuse.

Substance abuse may be either the cause or result of
other problems. Whatever the situation is, the problem
with alcohol and drugs must be dealt with first. The
student with a substance abuse problem will experience
difficulty in all areas of his or her life: school, friendships,
relationships, family, and health.

Sometimes a student may approach you, already
having surrendered to the fact he or she has a substance
abuse problem. In this case, the counselee has overcome
denial, which is the most deadly factor in alcoholism and
drug addiction. You will be able to listen to the counselee's
feelings and explain his or her options.

Symptoms of substance abuse are not the same for
each person. There are many unique situations and
variations according to the individual. Remember to use
your active listening skills and go to your supervisor
with any questions or doubts.

Depressants: depressants slow down or reduce physiological functions.

Common drugs abused	Street name(s)
Alcohol	Booze
Barbiturates	Downers, reds, barbs
Tranquilizers	Valium, Librium (brand names)
Marijuana	Pot, weed, grass, bud
Hashish	Hash
Methaqualone	Ludes, quads

Stimulants: stimulants speed up or increase physiological functions.

Common drugs abused	Street name(s)
Amphetamines	Speed, whites, uppers
Cocaine	Coke, blow, snow, white, crack
Nicotine	Cigarettes, smokes

Hallucinogenics: hallucinogens and psychedelics cause major distortion of thoughts and senses. They produce a psychosis-like state of mind, characterized by visual hallucinations.

Common drugs abused	Street name(s)
Lysergic acid deithylamide	LSD, acid
Psilocybin	magic mushrooms, 'shrooms
Phencyclidine	PCP, angel dust

Narcotics: opiates or narcotic analgesics decrease pain.
Use of these results in euphoria, decrease in breathing
rate, pain relief, and physical dependence.

Common drugs abused	Street name(s)
Morphine	Morphine
Methylmorphine	Codeine
Diacetylmorphine	Heroin

Symptoms of substance abuse:

Physical indicators:
- alcohol on breath
- sudden weight loss or gain
- poor complexion
- hyperactivity
- sluggishness
- change in pupil size
- sleep disturbances

Symptoms resulting or relating directly from abuse:
- increase in use
- dependency
- inability to control use
- change in the type of substance used
- preoccupation with drugs and alcohol
- blackouts
- serious consequences from use, i.e. drunk driv-
  ing or drunk in public arrests

Personality characteristics and feelings:
- mood swings

- depression
- anger
- unreliability
- irritability
- defensiveness
- lying
- isolation

Symptoms relating to school, friends, and social habits
- change in peer group
- change in dress or grooming habits
- drop in attendance at school
- drop in grades
- change in financial status
- rebellious attitude and delinquent acting out
- loss of interest in school or extracurricular activities

Steps for the peer counselor:

When counselee is in denial:
- Help the counselee look at the effect of the substance abuse on his or her life.
- Work with the counselee in defining the problem.
- When serious consequences are occurring, talk to your peer counseling supervisor.

When the counselee has admitted a substance abuse problem:
- Discuss options for recovery.

- Ask the counselee what he or she wants to do.
- Make an appropriate referral.

Things to keep in mind:

- Always deal with the counselee's feelings.
- You will be unable to successfully work with the counselee on any other issues while he or she is still abusing alcohol and drugs.
- The substance abuser will feel hopeless, powerless, and frustrated in his or her life. He or she may feel there is no way to change oneself or the life situations around him or her.

Where to refer the counselee:

- Alcoholics Anonymous.
- Narcotics Anonymous.
- Cocaine Anonymous.
- A recovering alcoholic/addict you know personally or through your peer counseling class.
- A substance abuse program at your school (not all schools have this).
- A counselor, psychologist, psychotherapist, or psychiatrist — preferably one who works with alcoholics/addicts regularly.
- Drug and alcohol dependency unit — inpatient.
- Drug and alcohol dependency center — outpatient.

TEENAGE PREGNANCY

The United States is experiencing an epidemic of teen pregnancies—more than any other industrialized nation. The results of this epidemic for teenagers include poverty, curtailed education, and greater physical risks for the young mother and her child.

Facts (Source: U. S. Department of Health and Human Services):

- Four out of every ten teenage girls will become pregnant at least once before they are twenty years old.
- The younger the mother, the more likely she is to have complications from pregnancy. These might include anemia, toxemia, or a miscarriage.
- The younger the mother, the more likely her baby will have a low birth weight, which is a major cause of infant mortality. Her baby also is more likely to suffer from birth defects and mental retardation than the baby who is born to a woman who is older.
- Only half of all teen mothers finish high school.
- Teen mothers who marry are three times more likely to be separated or divorced within 15 years than are the women who wait until they are in their twenties to have children.
- Two-thirds of families headed by teen mothers exist below the poverty level.

As a peer counselor, you may be called upon to help young women who are pregnant or who think they are. You must deal with your own feelings on this issue in order to remain objective. If you are not comfortable with the issue of pregnancy, you may choose to refer the counselee to a different peer counselor.

Considerations to keep in mind when counseling pregnant teens:

- The counselee may have conflicting feelings.
- The counselee often does not know what to do.
- She may reach out to you for assistance and support.
- Remember to help the counselee deal with her feelings.
- Encourage the counselee to reach out to other people in her life for support.
- You may want to refer the counselee to the school counselor, mental health professional, or minister for further guidance and an exploration of options.

CHAPTER 7

MOTIVATION

Becoming a peer counselor is like any other new experience. It is exciting, challenging, interesting, and rewarding. This initial thrill may not last indefinitely. There may come times when you are tired, depressed, burned-out, or unmotivated. Do not feel guilty. Your feelings are perfectly normal. You may need some time away from counselees. During your rest period, take time for yourself. You may use this time to regroup and revitalize—and to see where you are with your own feelings.

During your time of reflection, concentrate on your successes, not on your apparent failures. Situations which may have seemed unsuccessful to you may have planted seeds which will blossom sometime in the future. You may hear about them later, or you may never know the important contribution you have made to someone's life. Just keep in mind that the more counselees you see, the more successes you will have— and by the law of statistics, more failures also. Professional counselors recognize the fact that they cannot help everyone they see. They know they will have some failures. You will also have some failures. Do not feel guilty about them. Do the very best job that you can do; refer to a professional when you cannot handle a situation; and feel good about what you have accomplished.

You, the peer counselor, are a very special person. You fill a spot which is unique. Other people will come to you for help because they will recognize those qualities in you which they admire and respect. They will see your concern and caring for people of all races, economic status and cultural heritage. You will be recognized as a nonjudgmental person who does not stereotype a person because of his or her physical appearances, abilities, values, or ethnic origins. Your dedication and endurance for sticking with a counselee through "thick and thin" will be noticed and appreciated. You will model certain behavior which you will want to see developed in your counselee—he or she will see the respect you have for yourself and the value you place on your own high self-esteem. You will radiate the love you have for all people who are experiencing many kinds of problems and life situations.

In summary: you are a peer counselor because you care and are concerned; you accept and do not judge; you show dedication and endurance; you model self-awareness and high self-esteem; you radiate love. How fortunate your counselee is to have you as a peer counselor. How special you are!

Listen

When I ask you to listen to me and you start giving advice you have not done what I asked.

When I ask you to listen to me and you begin to tell me why I shouldn't feel that way, you are trampling on my feelings.

When I ask you to listen to me and you feel you have to do something to solve my problem, you have failed me, strange as that may seem.

Listen!! All I asked, was that you listen. Not to talk or do — just hear me.

Advice is cheap; 10 cents will get both Dear Abby and Billy Graham in the same newspaper.

And I can do for myself; I'm not helpless.

But, when you accept as a simple fact that I do feel what I feel no matter how irrational, then I can quit trying to convince you and get about the business of understanding what's behind this irrational feeling. And when that's clear, the answers are obvious and I don't need advice.

Irrational feelings make sense when we understand what's behind them.

Perhaps that's why prayer works, sometimes, for people because God is mute, and he doesn't give advice or try to fix things. He just listens and lets you work it out for yourself.

So please, listen and just hear me. And, if you want to talk, wait a minute for your turn; and I'll listen to you.

Anonymous

BIBLIOGRAPHY

Alberti, Robert E., Ph.D. and Michael L. Emmons, Ph.D.
        Your Perfect Right: A Guide to Assertive Living. San
        Luis Obispo, California: Impact Publishers, 1985.
Anonymous. *Alcoholics Anonymous.* New York: Alcoholics
        Anonymous World Services, Inc., 1987.
Boskind-White, M. and W. C. White, Jr. *Bulimarexia, The
        Binge/Purge Cycle.* New York: W.W. Norton and
        Company, 1988.
Bower, Sharon and Gordon Bower. *Asserting Yourself.*
        Reading, Massachusetts: Addison-Wesley, 1976.
Brammer, Lawrence. *The Helping Relationship: Process and
        Skills.* Englewood Cliffs, New Jersey: Prentice-
        Hall, 1973.
Bruch, H. *The Golden Cage: The Enigma of Anorexia Nervosa.*
        Cambridge, Massachusetts: Harvard University
        Press, 1978.
Carkhuff, Robert R. *The Art of Helping VI.* Amherst,
        Massachusetts: Human Resource Development
        Press, Inc., 1987.
Carroll, Charles R. *Drugs in Modern Society.* Dubuque,
        Iowa: Wm. C. Brown Publishers, 1985.
D'Andrea, Vincent and Peter Salovey. *Peer Counseling
        Skills and Perspectives.* Palo Alto, California:
        Science and Behavior Books, 1983.
Egan, Gerald. *You and Me: The Skills of Communicating and
        Relating To Others.* Monterey, California: Brooks/
        Cole Publishing Company, 1977.
Egan, Gerald. *The Skilled Helper,* third edition. Monterey,
        California: Brooks/Cole Publishing Company,
        1986.

Furstenberg, F., Jr., J. Menken and R. Lincoln. *Teenage Sexuality, Pregnancy, and Childbearing.* Philadelphia: University of Pennsylvania Press, 1981.

Garfinkel, P. E. and Garner, D. M. *Anorexia Nervosa: A Multidimensional Perspective.* New York: Brunner/Mazel, 1982.

Gray, H.D. and J. Tindall. *Peer Counseling: In-depth Look at Training Peer Helpers.* Muncie, Indiana: Accelerated Development, 1985.

Johnston, L.D., J. G. Bachman and P.M. O'Malley. *Highlights from Student Drug Use in America 1975-1981.* U.S. Department of Health and Human Services, Public Health Service, National Institute on Drug Abuse, 1982.

Kennedy, Eugene. *Crisis Counseling: The Essential Guide for Nonprofessional Counselors.* New York: Continuum Publishing Company, 1986.

Kubler-Ross, Elizabeth. *On Death and Dying.* New York: MacMillan Publishing Company, 1969.

Levenkron, S. *Treating and Overcoming Anorexia Nervosa.* New York: Warner Books, 1982.

Loughary, W. John and Theresa M. Ripley. *Helping Others Help Themselves.* New York: McGraw-Hill, 1979.

MacFarlane, Kee and Jill Waterman with Shawn Conerly, Linda Damon, Michael Durfee, and Suzanne Long. *Sexual Abuse of Young Children.* New York: Guilford Publications, Inc., 1986.

Moore, Joseph. *A Teen's Guide to Ministry.* Liguori, Missouri: Liguori Publications, 1988.

Myrick, Robert D. and Tom Ervey. *Caring and Sharing.* Minneapolis, Minnesota: Educational Media Corporation, 1984.

Myrick, Robert D. and Tom Ervey. *Youth Helping Youth.* Minneapolis, Minnesota: Education Corporation, 1985.

Myrick, Robert D. and Don L. Sorenson. *Peer Helping: A Practical Guide.* Minneapolis, Minnesota: Educational Media Corporation, 1988.

Peck, M.L. *Youth Suicide.* New York: Springer Publishers, 1985.

Phillips, Maggie. *The Peer Counseling Training Course.* San Jose, California: Resource Publishers, 1990.

Riebel, Linda K., Ph.D. *Understanding Eating Disorders: A Guide for Healthcare Professionals.* Sacramento, California: Robert D. Anderson Publishing Company, 1988.

Rogers, Carl R. *On Becoming A Person.* Boston, Massachusetts: Houghtin-Mifflin Company, 1961.

Satir, Virginia. *Self-Esteem.* Milbrae, California: Celestial Arts, 1975.

Sturkie, Joan. *Listening With Love: True Stories From Peer Counseling.* San Jose, California: Resource Publishers, 1987.

Sturkie, Joan and Gordon R. Bear. *Christian Peer Counseling: Love In Action.* Dallas, Texas: Word, Inc., 1989.

Sturkie, Joan and Dr. Alisann Frank. *Teachers' Guide to Listening With Love.* San Jose, California: Resource Publishers, 1989.

Sturkie, Joan and Marsh Cassady. *Acting It Out: 74 Short Plays for Starting Discussions with Teenagers.* San Jose, California:Resource Publishers, 1990.

Van Cleave, Stephen, Walter Bryd and Kathy Revell, *Counseling for Substance Abuse and Addiction.* Waco, Texas: Word Books, 1987.

Van Ornum, William and John B. Mordock. *Crisis Counseling With Children and Adolescents: A Guide for Non-professional Counselors.* New York: Continuum Publishing Company, 1983.

Varenhorst, Barbara. *Real Friends.* San Francisco: Harper and Row, 1983.

Varenhorst, Barbara with Lee Sparks. *Training Teenagers for Peer Ministry.* Loveland, Colorado: Group Books, 1988.

Wallerstein, J. S. and J. B. Kelly. *Surviving the Breakup: How Children and Parents Cope with Divorce.* New York: Basic Books, 1980.

Revised and Expanded Edition!

New Teacher's Guide Available!

Listening With Love
True Stories from Peer Counseling
By Joan Sturkie

270 pages, 6"x9",
  $9.95 paperbound
ISBN 0-89390-150-4

270 pages, 6"x9",
  $16.95 clothbound
ISBN 0-89390-151-2

64 pages, 5 ½"x 8 ½", $9.95
teacher's guide ISBN 0-89390-161-X

Joan Sturkie tells you how young people have helped each other overcome problems related to drugs, sexuality, divorce, abuse, communication, and low self-esteem. Expanded edition includes section on how to start and maintain such a program, letters from the original students who went through the peer counseling program, and an expanded bibliography.

The separate teacher's guide, written by a prominent educator, makes *Listening With Love* easy to use as a text for a peer counseling course. It includes an opening "lecturette," questions for post-reading, activity suggestion, and a brief promo to prepare for the next lesson.

You Can Help Troubled Teenagers!

THE PEER
COUNSELING
TRAINING
COURSE

by Maggie Phillips

The Peer Counseling Training Course is a teacher's guide and complete curriculum for a junior high or high school course in peer counseling. This course helps you train teens to be there for each other. It is divided into sixteen units. Units one through nine introduce students to the skills they must learn to become good counselors. Units ten through sixteen deal with specific problems the student counselors might face, such as peer pressure, drugs, drinking, etc.

This curriculum was formerly known as the H.O.L.D. program from the Pajaro Valley Unified School District in Watsonville, California.

The Peer Counseling Training Course
by Maggie Phillips
revised by Joan Sturkie
Loose leaf $49.95, 126 pages, 8½" x 11"
ISBN 0-89390-185-7

Difficult Topic?

Use *Acting It Out* to start the discussion.

ACTING IT OUT: 74 Short Plays for Starting Discussions with Teenagers
by Joan Sturkie and Marsh Cassady
Paperbound $21.95, 357 pages, 6" x 9"
ISBN 0-89390-178-4
Use these 74 short plays with teenagers to explore the serious problems that affect their lives, from anorexia to sexual abuse to suicide. Each drama can be performed as is or continued spontaneously. There are discussion questions at the end of each drama. Ideal for classes in peer counseling, for group counseling situations, or for youth ministry.

Excerpt from a play about sexual abuse:

Barbara: I should have suspected, but I didn't. Looking back, I see that he started paying a lot more attention to me six months or so before this happened. He was always a loving man with Mom and Peter and me. But when he kissed me, it was just a little too long. When he hugged me, I'd start to feel uncomfortable and try to pull away. But he acted hurt, so I didn't make a big deal out of it.

Dixie: Look, Barbara, someone's going to have to report this. You realize that, don't you?

Barbara: I know. But then what? What's going to happen to my family?

To order see the order form on the next page.